Winnie & Ruby's Folsom ABC Adventure

Featuring

Adventure Awaits!

Winnie - The Sutter Street Pig

Ruby - Ruby's Books

To Alexander and Amy —
Ruby is waiting to meet you!

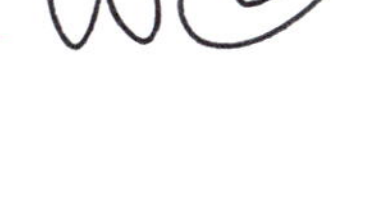

Written and Illustrated by Brian Wallace

For
Jessica, Cole and Claire

Winnie & Ruby's Folsom ABC Adventure
Written and Illustrated by Brian Wallace
Edited by Jessica Wallace
Published by Newport Press
ISBN-13: 978-0-57-836884-9

All rights reserved. No part of this book may be reproduced or transmitted in any form or by any means, electronic or mechanical, including photocopying, recording, or by an information storage and retrieval system - except by a reviewer who may quote brief passages in a review to be printed in a magazine or newspaper - without permission in writing from the publisher.

Copyright © 2022 by Brian Wallace | www.brianwallaceart.com

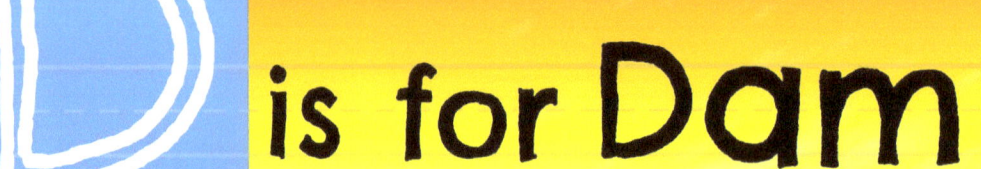

D is for Dam

The dam holds the water in Folsom Lake.
When the lake fills up, the gates open and water flows down the river.

E is for Electricity

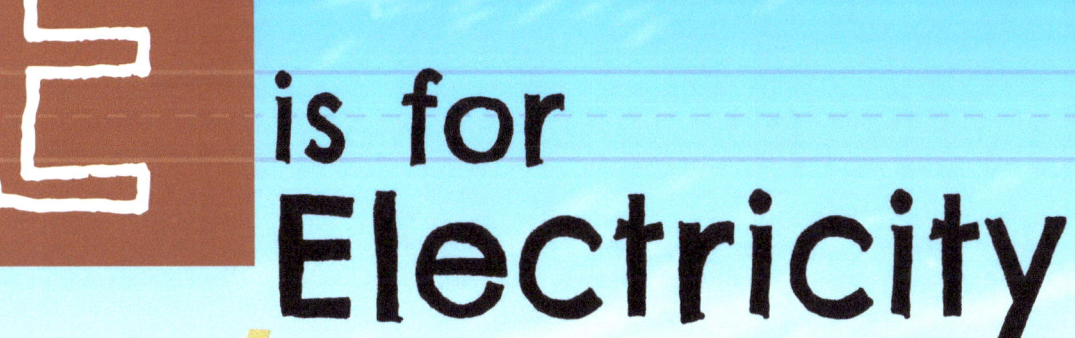

The historic Folsom Powerhouse used water to create electricity.
You can go inside the brick building and see the huge generators. Exciting!

F is for Farmers' Market

It is fun to find fresh fruits and vegetables at the Farmers' Market. Winnie has her favorites! What are yours?

G is for Goats

Goats gather to graze on grass in the summer.
Ruby thinks they are great fun to watch!

I is for Ice Skating

The ice skating rink is a winter tradition. Skate on the invigorating ice around the railroad turntable.

J is for Johnny Cash

I Hear the Train A-Comin'

You can't talk about Folsom without mentioning Johnny Cash. His song *Folsom Prison Blues* is known all over the world!

K is for Kayak

Kicking back in a kayak is a fun way to explore Lake Natoma. Kids and adults love the cool water on a hot Folsom summer day.

M is for Mansion

The stately Cohn mansion looks majestic in the moonlight. The house was built in 1890s and sits atop Folsom's "Nob Hill."

N is for Nisenan

Ruby and Winnie imagine what it might have been like when the Nisenan people lived in harmony with the land.

Q is for Quail

Quail scurry quickly when walkers and cyclists pass by.
The California quail is the state bird of California.

S is for Sutter Street

A stroll down Sutter Street in the summer may lead you to a sweet treat. It appears that Winnie may have found something scrumptious.

T is for Trails

Time to take a walk on the trails. Walk in the shade of trees and be on the lookout for wild turkeys.

U is for Underground

Rumor has it that there are underground tunnels beneath Sutter Street. Be careful, Winnie and Ruby!

V is for Volunteer

Winnie lends a helping hand (or snout). It's great to volunteer! You can work with others on projects that beautify the city.

W is for Waterslide

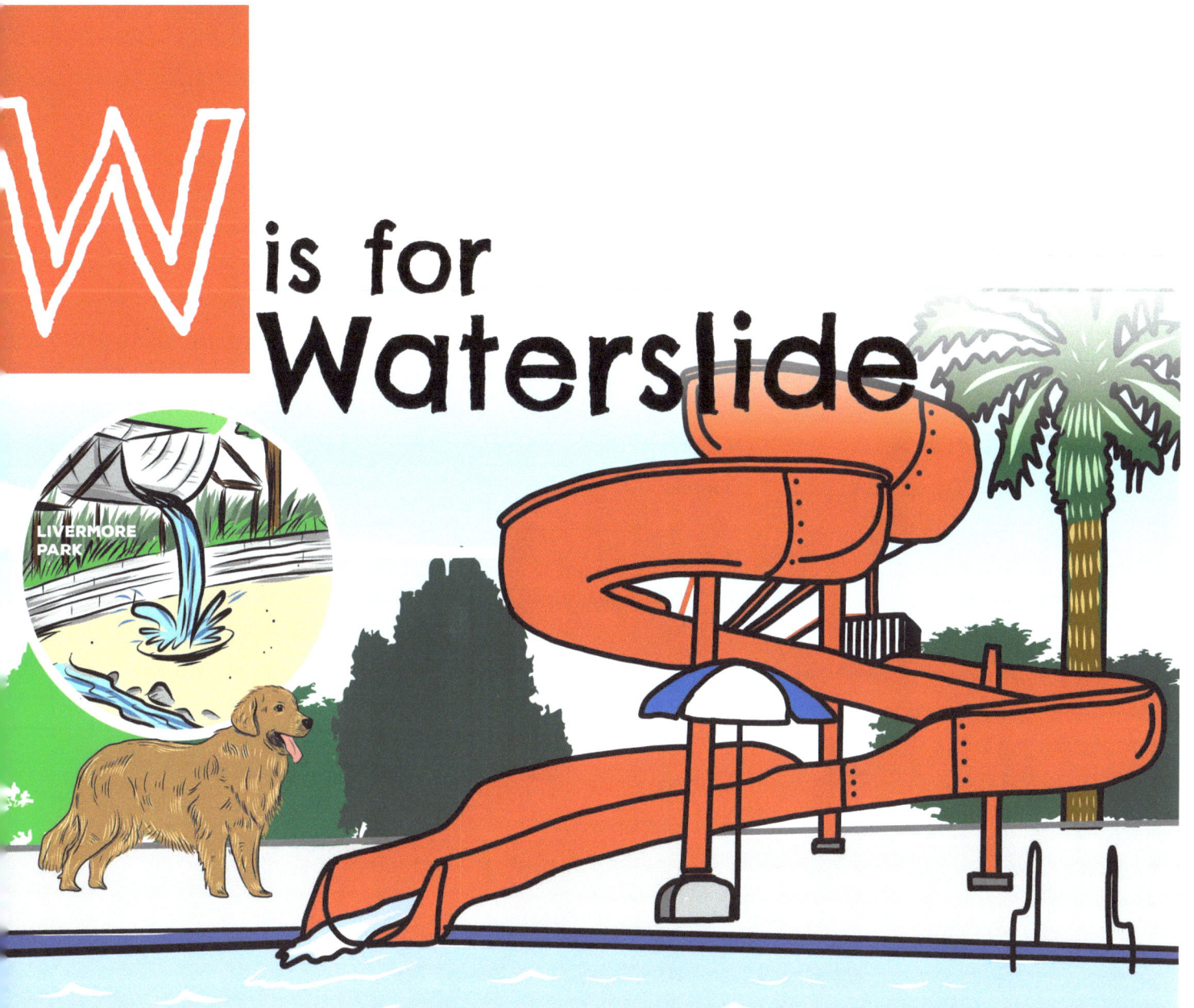

Ruby watches kids whisk down the winding waterslide. If you want to cool down in the summer, wander over to the many water features in Folsom parks.

X is for Xylophone

Winnie goes to hear the Folsom Symphony. The xylophone makes an interesting sound when the musician strikes the wooden bars with the mallet.

Y is for Yee Haw!

Yee Haw! The western traditions in Folsom run deep. When the rodeo comes to town, it's time to put on your boots and cowboy hat.

Z is for Zoo Sanctuary

Rosie the Donkey

Hello, Friends!

Bernie the Raccoon

The Folsom City Zoo Sanctuary is home to many rescued animals. Winnie stops by to say hello to Bernie and Rosie.

The Real Ruby and Winnie!

Folsom, California

A is for Adventure: Winnie and Ruby start their adventure on the Johnny Cash trail. The pedestrian bridge behind them is the Johnny Cash Bridge that crosses over Lake Natoma Crossing.

B is for Bicycle: There are over 50 miles of trails in Folsom. The Johnny Cash Trail is accessible from the Historic District and connects to several popular bile trails around Folsom.

C is for Candy: Snook's Chocolate Factory has been making candy in Folsom since 1963.

D is for Dam: The Folsom Dam was built in 1955. It is 340 ft. high and 1,400 ft. tall.

E is for Electricity: In 1895, the Folsom Powerhouse used water from the American River to produce electricity, which was sent to Sacramento 22 miles away. The Powerhouse is now a State Historic Park and open to the public.

F is for Farmers' Market: The Farmers' Market is open year-round.

G is for Goats: In the summer, goats are used to eat dried grass and maintain open space.

H is for History: Folsom has a rich history. The western terminus of Pony Express is right in the Historic District. Miners also came to Folsom in search of gold!

I is for Ice Skating: The ice rink has become a popular winter tradition in Folsom.

J is for Johnny Cash: Johnny Cash was a famous American singer-songwriter that released a song called *Folsom Prison Blues* in December 1955. The song is known all over the world.

K is for Kayak: Kayakers and paddleboarders love Lake Natoma. Lake Natoma prohibits motorized watercraft, and the lake is dammed, so the water is generally very still and peaceful.

L is for Lake: Folsom Lake is a great place for boating, fishing, biking, hiking and so much more. Folsom Lake State Recreation Area is open to the public year-round.

M is for Mansion: The Cohn Mansion is one of Folsom's most unique homes. It was built by local businessman and State Senator, Phillip Cohn in the 1890s.

N is for Nisenan: The Nisenan are the indigenous people that have called Folsom home for thousands of years.

O is for Oak Trees: Native oak trees in Folsom date back hundreds of years and grow in public areas and the backyards of Folsom residents. These trees have historical significance and are protected.

P is for Piano: A public piano can be found on Sutter Street. The piano was donated and everyone is invited to play it!

Q is for Quail: Quail are often seen on trails throughout Folsom. They usually nest on the ground.

R is for Railroad: The Sacramento Valley Railroad was the first transit railroad in California. On February 22, 1856, the first train left Old Sacramento and terminated in Folsom.

S is for Sutter Street: Historic Sutter Street offers a step back in time. Admire the architecture while shopping, eating, and exploring.

T is for Trails: There are several trails in Folsom. Bikers, walkers and runners enjoy the Humbug-Willow Creek Trail, Folsom Rail Trail, Folsom Lake Trail, and Oak Parkway Trail. Remember, bike on the right side of the trail and walk on the left side.

U is for Underground: There is an underground tunnel 10 feet below Sutter Street that is 120 feet long. According to people who have seen it, it is dark, musty and wet.

V is for Volunteer: Many Folsom residents participate in Folsom Community Service Day, which brings together thousands of volunteers for one day of service projects.

W is for Waterslide: The waterslide at the Folsom Aquatic Center is fun for kids of all ages. Many Folsom parks also have water features that are fun places to cool down during the hot Folsom summer.

X is for Xylophone: Folsom celebrates art and culture. Enjoy the arts and a symphony with a xylophone player.

Y is for Yee Haw: Western traditions, such as the annual 4th of July rodeo, are deeply rooted in Folsom's history.

Z is for Zoo Sanctuary: The Folsom Zoo Sanctuary opened in 1963 and is the home to hundreds of animals from squirrels and deer to bobcats and bears. The zoo is safe haven for many rescued animals.

 95630

Special Thanks to:
Winnie and the Felts Family
Ruby and the Gould Family
The Folsom History Museum / Folsom Historical Society
Christine Brainerd
Judy Collinsworth

ALSO AVAILABLE FROM NEWPORT PRESS

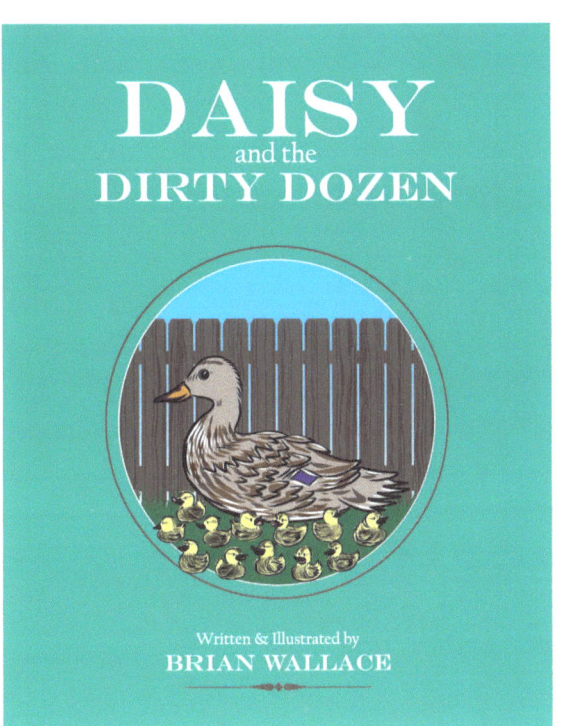

Daisy and the Dirty Dozen
Written and Illustrated by Brian Wallace

Daisy and the Dirty Dozen is the true and heartwarming story of a mallard duck and her 12 ducklings that take up residence in a suburban family's swimming pool.

The Wallace family take the 13 ducks "under their wing" and are able to watch a mother duck care for her ducklings right from their kitchen window.

The ducks also provide the Wallace family with the opportunity to learn more about wildlife and how to enjoy sharing their yard with a family of ducks.

You can see the real-life Daisy and the Dirty Dozen at www.daisyandthedirtydozen.com

CPSIA information can be obtained
at www.ICGtesting.com
Printed in the USA
BVHW020914110422
633265BV00002B/5